UNDER A COMMON SKY

AND OTHER SHORT POEMS

NAVEEN BALA

Copyright © Naveen Bala
All Rights Reserved.

This book has been published with all efforts taken to make the material error-free after the consent of the author. However, the author and the publisher do not assume and hereby disclaim any liability to any party for any loss, damage, or disruption caused by errors or omissions, whether such errors or omissions result from negligence, accident, or any other cause.

While every effort has been made to avoid any mistake or omission, this publication is being sold on the condition and understanding that neither the author nor the publishers or printers would be liable in any manner to any person by reason of any mistake or omission in this publication or for any action taken or omitted to be taken or advice rendered or accepted on the basis of this work. For any defect in printing or binding the publishers will be liable only to replace the defective copy by another copy of this work then available.

Thank you...

Almighty, for everything you bestowed upon me.

Rupul, for being the soul of my existence and turning me into a
different person.

Maa, Baba, for your neverending love.

Mama, Ria, Siddhu, for being the family I needed but never had.

A special thanks to the Friends I earned and lost on this journey
called Life.

Contents

Contents

Contents

Contents

Contents

Preface

This book is a compilation of thoughts, dreams, and experiences. The poems are memories of good and bad days and depict heartfelt emotions.

Over the years life will surprise you with its fair share of ups and downs. You may encounter multiple situations and scenarios that are either peaceful or compel you to react in a certain way. You might as well be fortunate enough to meet a few people who come across as beacons of hope and positivity. So take every downfall as a lesson, every affirmation as a trophy, and decorate your memory palace. Whenever in doubt visit this palace and strengthen your will. Be rest assured, circumstances will take a right turn.

This book is based upon an assurance that no matter whatever the situation is or wherever your soulmates are, you share a common sky, a common dream. This book is my memory palace.

1. To Rupul

I had a notion that I knew a lot about love,
It is you who taught me
that one who upholds stands all above.
Thank you for all the love, support, and positivity.
I am grateful for the times you had shown your patience with
me, for the times you turned things around.
Thanks for being who you are.
I am certain, one day we will conquer it all.

2. Under a Common Sky

•2•

I sit back, breath in, close my eyes,
I long for an embrace, wish to forever hold your hand,
and worth of the shared meals I realize.
We make new memories, relive the old,
The pictures by you or of yours, are pure bliss,
Hidden emotions unfold.
The day will surely come when we share the same roof,
For now, I feel blessed under a common sky.

3. Mother

• 3 •

Obliged for your support, for being there,
for all the non-mandatory love n care.
Despite my stupidity and actions that provoke,
You act as my magic wand, my invisibility cloak.
my shield for the relentless weather,
If I ever lose you, I'll repent forever.

4. Father

• 4 •

Filling colors in a million dreams,
only a few of them his own.
Being a wall, hiding behind one,
Seldom letting his thoughts known.
How does one keep the balance?
By himself or is one told?
Maybe someday I'll run into my guide,
Or might transform as I grow old.

5. Divine

What does it take to complete a Man?
Is this how each life is meant to be?
Endlessly searching within and around,
unanswered questions since eternity.
Faith saves me many times,
but I wonder how you function.
I assume time is not relatable for you,
Is it just about the law of attraction?
How does one be everywhere yet stay enigmatic,
But you will surely have your reasons.

6. Alive

My best friend and companion,
a crazy head at times.
For you, I write this out of love,
and make sure it rhymes.
Sitting and watching animated humans,
yet your thoughts run through my mind.
I submerge myself in your thoughts,
my love, you are one of a kind!

7. Awake

Moving around on my bed tired,
but with eyes wide open I stay awake.
I close my eyes to count the sheep,
and find myself floating on a lake.
something thing pulls me down,
Startled, I wake up and search you within.
Your thoughts calm me down,
as in our memories, I dive in.

8. Balance

A darker hue spilled over
taking all in as it spread.
I sit back and see the changing constants
while the globe gears up for a reset.
The struggle to balance good & bad, old & new
I find it within, I see it in you.

9. Beautiful

Mad, moody, on the edge at times
and with endless love.
You belong to my soul
my constant inspiration and Godsend.
I wish and pray desperately
for our dreams to come true.
As in my every thought
I wish to be beside you.

10. Black

Limitless it seems at times,
mark of the beginning and the end.
Still unsure about how,
and when he became such a good friend.
I unconsciously chose you,
for decisions big or small.
Thank you for bringing me luck.
Thank you for absorbing it all!

11. Blank

While staring at the window, my mind drifted away,
The head felt light, the soul regained its shine.
I was floating aimlessly in a certain happy place till
a certain storm cloud started chasing me.
I ran for life, tired, breathless, seeking help,
After a while, as my life started draining out, it consumed me.
I sprang from my sleeping state and sat upright,
puzzled by the visuals of my dream.
I turned around and checked, there was nobody in sight.
Wish someone would have asked if everything was alright.

12. Blessing

I search frantically,
getting restless by the second.
Waiting for a miracle
to declare your presence.
When suddenly wind flew in a beautiful flower,
as a blessing in disguise.
There was no end to my happiness then,
and the power of prayer I did realize.

13. Breathe

Constant rumbling in the background
and I sit to meditate.
On my most recent actions
I do an analysis and try to contemplate,
what went wrong to disturb my natural order.
Just then someone says "Relax, take a deep breath and don't bother,
as the world is supposed to move in a way
and our encounters are for our good I would say".

14. Broken

Breathing one at a time,
the beating is also slow.
One by one thing poke at me,
I take notice and let go.
What can I do that all come together?
How should I save the sail?
I will make do, I will try to.
But my promise to you is what I can't fail.

15. Butterfly

Asleep and changing by the second,
new identity & rebirth lost if you give in.
Motionless, dead on the outside,
endless turmoil within.
As you open your eyes chaos greets you,
between death & life, your mind goes back & forth.
A successful ordeal transforms you
into one of the most beautiful beings on Earth.

16. Calm

It is tough to not react,
to situations and circumstances surrounding you.
In the unending chaos,
the signs of hope might be very few.
Go ahead and try your best to remain composed,
and refrain from causing any harm.
If you can't escape, go through,
Conquer your fears and find your calm.

17. Captain

I got you as a friend, teacher, and guide,
in every low, you stood by my side.
Turning over a new leaf today,
when till yesterday I was blind.
I think I'll forever need your support,
I hope you don't mind.

18. Child

Ever tried to see the world
through a child's eyes?
What did you see when you were one?
Let me remind you of that time,
when you stopped to feel the breeze,
basked under the Sun.
Thoughts were few, redundant but light and pure.
Have you never wished to be a child once more?

19. Children of God

• 19 •

At least once take some time out and visit the children of God.

You will be pleased to meet the tiny beings with humongous hearts,

which beats in search of answers

to the numerous puzzles stored within.

Unknown of what the future holds for them,

slightly afraid, but no thoughts about giving in.

20. Choices

Sometimes I wonder is it the insect
who flies towards the fire,
and gets consumed by in return
foolish to listen to his inner greed and desire?
Or is he a saint who chooses fire
to purify the self, over old age or a predator's lair.

21. Cold

Words unspoken,
but rolling out of the eyes.
My eyes speak the truth,
and tongue weaves a new lie.
Choking inside I wish my life to end,
"Oh! It is nothing, just a cold my friend."

22. Darkness

A safety net is all we require,
made of love and helping hands.
A fortress is what heart desires,
guarded by people of varied blood yet our own.
Carbon turns a darker shade of black each day,
into unimaginable beings, each of us has grown.

23. Deserve

On the way to uncover a hidden treasure,
but the unknown of its contents,
you slowly tread on the strange land,
praying for your dream's existence.
At last, you face your fate and question yourself,
was it worth it to keep my dreams preserved?
Finally, you get far more than you wanted,
and exactly as you deserved.

24. Disabled

One of the pair was beaten up & crying,
other's dreams shattered.
Our false egos enclosed in tiny lifespan,
kills and leaves innocence battered.
True love embraced by God, shunned by Man,
This is where Hell actually began.

25. Distancing

• 25 •

Social media, social media,
Social distancing, I practice.
I pick up my phone to call/text,
and in my mind, create a list.
But it's been years since I said hello...
I take a pause and ponder solo.
Social media, social media,
Some social distancing, I practiced.

26. Disturbed

I wake up to the whispers of the night
& distorted dreams of soul in plight.
Not out of hunger, but the routine I feed.
Struggles of my life, or penance for my deed?
All the joys of life hanging by a thread.
Souls, loans, wishes will help me endure it till the end.

27. Divine

The world may be considered a bag of lies,
and us living beings as insignificant.
But does that line of thought help us?
Or make our present pleasant?
With partial truth is it right to form our prejudices,
and waste our limited time?
Instead, of cherishing the present,
helping each other for common progress is truly divine.

28. Dreams

What keeps the world spinning?
On which rhythm do you start your day?
Do you wish to achieve something in life?
Is something keeping you at bay?
Just believe in yourself, keep striving,
with an unfaltering focus on your goal.
Dreams are the reason for our existence,
The reason behind every hustle.

29. Emotions

Drawn to demise like the fireflies to fire!
Why can't one find a leash?
or a trap to contain the ill?
The emotions get hold of you,
and eventually, take you there,
no matter how strong one's will.
Just hold your fort and breathe.
Your focus will help you succeed.

30. Fear

There is a story running in the back
of our minds.
A story waiting to take control.
A plot that guides our thinking,
triggers an emotion, plays a negative role.
It teaches but limits our actions,
Nullifies our ability to reason.
We create the pits of our demise.
It makes a fool out of the wisest of the wise.

31. Forward March

• 31 •

Take a pause but ascend
Linger for a certain fall.
Struggle to set a foothold is real,
No effort can be branded as small.
Focus and march ahead, because each step is a win,
and you are meant to have it all.

32. Freedom

Wake up to the nth alarm,
drag yourself out of the bed.
Get ready for the outside world,
painfully chew a few morsels of bread.
Work is fun in itself,
excluding the unwanted weights attached.
People should be left free with a goal.
They are assigned containers instead.

33. Guide

Many minds, many thoughts,
Some carried love, darkness some brought
What to consider and which one to let go of?
If only a man could know!
One should follow one's heart.
Introspection is slow but a powerful start
Walk a certain distance alone and the vision will get clearer,
Darkness misguides only the souls who give in to fear.

34. Joy

• 34 •

Drastic actions after an emotional outburst,
Brain rushes in to isolate you from the pain.
Mistakes rattle, force you off course.
A chain of events crafting monsters you'll forever regret.
But today was a moment of joy after days of gloom,
all might not be lost yet.

35. Lonely

• 35 •

The excitement in the air,

as an important artist arrives for the fest.

A chance of interaction arose

out of a separate contest.

People excited and enthralled,

while mind asks to retreat.

The crowd makes me lonely,

I'd rather be happy retreating to an empty street.

36. Love

My world spins around you
Your thoughts make my days go by
Alone, the time comes to a standstill
In pair, the moments fly
I pray that you stay as you are
Fearless, adorned with a smile
Time spent with you makes me happy,
makes my pain worthwhile.

37. Family

Warm friendly souls
talking, suggesting, hovering around.
Part of one's good days,
In pain, they'll definitely be found.
Energy sponge with a rightful say.
Trust me, you wouldn't want it any other way!

38. Foundation

The World became difficult the moment I left your care,
which I willingly wanted to do for years.
Gave life, carried me through the storms,
Scolded me, loved & hid your tears.
I always forget, get angry, shout and fight.
I wish to one day make it all right.

39. Goals

• 39 •

Set your eyes on the goal,

imagine, and visualize the moment when you reach there.

How great are the joy and satisfaction?

So what is stopping you from springing into action?

Invite the World to your Kingdom and let them see,

Set your goals, to set yourself free.

40. Help

• 40 •

Leaves withered and flying around,
waiting at crossroads thinking where to go.
Would you take my hand, drag me a few steps?
Forcibly make me follow?
Lonely, painful is what I'm going through,
for your support, all my life I'll be indebted to you.

41. History

Today we share a common pain,
a chapter of time revisited.
Innocent souls butchered by the throne,
in the festival of false resolve.
For solving the problems created by our own,
whom should we involve?
Misery awaits the kingdom ruled by dim-witted
Today we share a common pain.

42. I Wish

I wish I held your hand,
I miss you and can't withstand
that the mistakes of my past,
unrightfully took your life.
You push me to be good,
the amount you love me no one could,
I had just killed your soul,
and your memories are keeping me alive.

43. Injustice

Blessed, never hurt a soul,
always searched for the good in all.
But one day an addiction got better of him,
and started his downfall.
The world forgot the good,
didn't stop to blame.
He wished to be healed,
but killed self out of shame.

44. Insanity

Disturbance in the air,
huge waves crashing in my mind.
Uncertainties of future worry me,
Neurons, conscience has gone blind.
I imagine and create the traps around me.
Is it my power to find flaws or just insanity?

45. Journey

The sands were once with the mountains,
inseparable, sticking together.
Then one by one they moved out,
surrendered to the atrocities of weather.
The penance freed them with a new struggle,
yet worth every drop of sweat.
They underwent an eye-opening journey
with endless struggle but no regret.

46. Jumble

• 46 •

Things are not the way it appears sometimes,
the World guides us as it chooses best.
Circumstances deviate us from the real,
human imagination spoils the rest.
It is okay to get deviated,
being harsh on self is never an answer.
Even the best of us deserve a break at times.

47. Kingdom

Half a month
of struggles, love, smiles, tears.
It takes courage to take ownership,
patience helps in working out our fears.
Your support helped me get through
and I promise to stay truthful to you.
I want to forever stay by your side,
build a kingdom of love to reside.

48. Life

• 48 •

I see you idling,
making sense of thoughts, sight, and sound
hiding from the world, waiting to be found.
Why don't we choose another game to play?
take some time out, together with spending the day.
Take a break for the Earth will go on.
The weight of the world need not be yours alone.

49. Lighthouse

• 49 •

Wish to wake up to your voice
talking, calling out my name.
Once the current storm passes,
the days are never gonna be the same.
I want to live that day, wish to hold you near.
You keep me human, calm my worst fears.

50. Longing

My morning spent waiting
for your call or just a sign.
I question should my baring of heart
considered a mistake of mine?
Desperate n restless, I text and call you
You must be occupied, but can't help as I miss you.

51. Lullaby

I sing to you and put you to sleep,

and you lie unconscious halfway through.

I wish everything got sorted at the same pace,

as how our friendship first grew.

The peaceful nights with your whispers as my lullaby,

I want them back and will endlessly try.

My morning spent waiting

for your call or just a sign.

I question should my baring of heart

considered a mistake of mine?

Desperate n restless, I text and call you

You must be occupied, but can't help as I miss you.

52. Magic

Simple moments of joy
carved out of the chaotic world.
The power to imagine a bright and new tomorrow
when the present is in pain and growing old.
We have the power to change our present
to generate warmth in hearts gone cold.

53. Marvel

Lying still on the bed of the ocean,
thinking how skillful and generous is the creator,
to have built such marvels with pure heart,
and left for us to play unmonitored.
But we act like an eclipse to our existence,
exploiting and ending day by day life's essence.

54. Memories

• 54 •

Signs awakened some dormant memories,
some forgotten emotions got triggered,
broke free and mesmerized the self
as tears rolled down and the present shivered,
with the appearance of joy from the core of my heart
The mind attained bliss as the day got a beautiful start.

55. Mesmerized

A soothing breeze glides around
traversing in random lanes.
Memories triggered of our time together
the words, scent, sound.
I long for your love so much
my actions lose their speed.
Mesmerized I lose track of time
heart flutters, flies around.

56. Mine

It has been a day of faith, prayers,
with little ups & downs.
With a little patience lost
& lots of moments of love found.
I really wish you were just an
arm's length apart to cuddle, to tease.
Together in love, we'll face life with a smile,
Will you be mine forever, please?

57. Morning

Standing on the balcony,

my eyes scan the breadth of the land.

Fresh, cold air fills the lungs,

I ponder with a cup of coffee in my hand.

Why is Man prone to outbursts?

Why does impulse take control of reason?

Wouldn't it be nice to perpetually rejoice?

Why do there have to be droughts and floods in a season?

I am nervous about making promises anew,

There is nothing good about the morning without you.

58. Motivation

Things are going to find a way through,
reach out, pull yourself up!
You are stronger than your best imagination,
keep aside the thoughts of giving up.
Why be afraid when you are capable of winning a war?
You are not alone even if you think you are.

59. Nature

A day full of excitement with an eagerness,
to complete what started long back.
A busy day full of moments,
that evaluate you, put you off track.
Things work for you always when you allow.
In weird ways, nature has your back somehow.

60. Oblivion

With open eyes, I meditate
recreate the existence around me.
I set up, fine-tune, redesign,
in the memories of you, I try to find myself.
Together we paint, draw, sketch, run around,
cook, form a band.
I wish I could show you,
how the World appears from where I stand.

61. Opinion

• 61 •

Do you get confused by suggestions?
Or refrain from giving any?
What is offered is many times biased
unlike claimed otherwise by many.
Don't worry,
keep your mind clear and then ask a query.
Let me tell you, my friend
The thing is, at the end
anything we say to others or do,
is for establishing our point of view.

62. Orange

A drink I love from the woman I love,
captured forever in my memory.
Not many days have gone by,
but the uncertainty is what is killing me.
In all the chaos, and newness,
some details like the cup's design,
I might misplace or take time to find.
But the vibrant wall will be etched in my mind.

63. Outshine

• 63 •

Excited, tensed about tomorrow,
It is tough to imagine myself in your shoes.
May you have the patience & perseverance
to crack the test, face the blues.
In the toughest of times, ourselves we shouldn't undermine.
Just be yourself & you'll outshine!

64. Patience

Days evolve into months and years,
certain instances relived each day.
Days of pain, of the scorching sun,
of rainbow hues and endless fun.
Perfection, flaws, situations anew,
just wish to be there with you.

65. Pause

• 65 •

My life was on pause.
The reason was because
of the time I found but missed you
Life took a turn and restarted.
I reached where I had departed,
and promised self to never
again make the mistake of leaving you.

66. Peach

Cute, beautiful, angelic,
Easy to read, challenging to interpret.
Multiple entities packaged as one,
stern as a teacher yet infinite doses of fun.
It would be lovely to always be there for you,
to enjoy your surprises, to try things new.
I relive and cherish our interactions,
It brightens my day seeing you smile.

67. Pebbles

Once a part of a mighty landscape
in search of an adventure,
they rush downriver.
Tough and unbound at the start,
they disintegrate by the second.
How to control when you can't maneuver?
When your heart aches keep your calm,
Just remember love is the key
and will be your strength forever.

68. Persistence

One good sign as we start our day,
taking us closer to our goals.
Inching closer with persistence,
while the Universe plays its role.
It feels so good when efforts get paid,
The fruits of labor are sweeter when delayed.

69. Power

Countless invisible lines are drawn,
countless concealed filters applied.
Measures are taken to forcibly prove the depth,
voices silenced if replied.
Age or money shouldn't define our worth.
One's choice of peace should solely be his own.
Yet power is widely respected and sought,
truth ignored, reasoning hidden in the unknown.

70. Presence

Captured every moment but feels
incomplete until I share.
Can't stop imagining us, I feel
your presence everywhere.
Only if the days rolled fast,
I know this uncertainty will end and our story last.

71. Promise

• 71 •

Invisible strings tie me up over and over
no matter how much I try to get free.
I keep the World's views aside,
but what to do when you say I'm not me.
I'll stand up as I want to conquer for us,
I promise to accept all challenges thus.

72. Purpose

How do you reach the end?
or find a new beginning?
When all you know is that you have a hidden purpose,
but every time you discover a new way of losing.
But strong-willed you push back on,
How dare fate distract God's own Son!

73. Realize

Sleep-deprived; I find it difficult
to open my eyes.
I've been having nightmares
of lost existence, dark skies.
On waking up I long for you
wish to hear from you.
As I cherish your presence in each day of struggle
what I was missing I realize.

74. Recovery

Slow & steady the days roll away
as we get busy collecting smiles & tears.
Wish could make a few moments stay.
Just a few drops from the endless years.
As those memories keep us anchored to our best.
They save us from our worst fears.

75. Rejoined

• 75 •

Blessed is the one who floats
with his eyes closed and thoughts on self and soul,
and all the obstacles somehow act in resonance
by stopping him to lead him to the goal,
where they all meditate as one
and become formless as when the life had begun.

76. Remember?

Remember the days of uncertainty,
the days of stress, anguish, and pain?
Thinking of what'll happen next,
we grew tense, prayed such conflicts never occurred again.
But I knew from the inside,
things will turn in our favor like always.
I just want you to come back fully one day,
We'll smile again remembering these days.

77. Remedy

The flower of love blossomed,
in a thousand years.
Heart flutters with joy,
eyes are full of tears.
The force lost is somehow regained
by endless cuts and sacrifice.
A remedy can never surpass prevention,
and is adopted by truly wise.

78. Repentance

• 78 •

With great pain, I take help of my pen,
How did I make a fool of myself again?
An action blew a happy portrait apart,
When the intention was to protect it from start.
Eyes stay moist, the heart feels dry,
shivering doesn't stop and you can't cry.
The curse acts in full even after endless repentance,
Death might be sweeter than any current instance.

79. Revive

I've been willingly crying out aloud,
to make you listen and draw you out.
because I can't stay another second apart,
from you without churning my heart
into a thousand pieces of memories and dreams
getting erased by the second into gut-wrenching screams
muffled when you picked me up just in time
and revived me. Now I surely know I'll be fine.

80. Run

The world's crashing,
tears rolling down the eyes.
Prayers stick to lips,
but will that suffice?
Signs and alarms ignored,
how can humanity wish to wake up?
But it'll only hold you till you breakout,
just keep running and you'll keep up.

81. Savior

Standing on the hill to get a clear picture,
instead, I witness a blurred sight.
Terrified, I repent as wrongs made unconsciously
don't make them right.
It would be so easy if I just jumped
maybe get a fresh start over.
But that wouldn't cure me as much,
as just then you hold my hand and pull me closer.

82. Shine

It is easy to
get lost in the crowd,
get pushed around,
get deprived of the basic respect,
and yet not get noticed by people around.
It is easy to
accept defeat than to fight,
be submissive than to stand for your right,
wander than to keep your goal in sight.
But no matter whatever the circumstance,
If you stay true to yourself you will be fine.
Focus on your goals and don't lose your shine.

83. Signs

A day at a time, a breath a second,
a name comes to mind.
A sweet whisper by a soul, God sent,
rejuvenates my heart.
All I have now are dreams of tomorrow,
Waiting for a revival, a life to start.

84. Sins

• 84 •

Braver today but the journey is long still,
We have to conquer mountains but first, let us climb a hill.
Your support acts like a spell,
I feel calm even when I am burning in hell.
Who keeps a count of the stabs to heart each day?
Can the end only ensure that sins are washed away?

85. Sister

• 85 •

A pure form of love and care,
a soul you reach out to, in despair.
A prime example of selflessness,
relation of unsaid understandings
an unbreakable bond shaped with and
out of childhood fights and stress.
Whom the soul searches for in intense and mindless
conversations,
in times of every need,
Having one in life is a blessing indeed.

86. Smile

Nothing as beautiful as a smile on your lips.
It just brightens up my day.
Your face speaks a thousand words in our video calls,
even if nothing you say.
Sometimes I just am happy imagining
you with me and then when I look at you.
No one will love me the way you do.
Braver today but the journey is long still,
We have to conquer mountains but first, let us climb a hill.
Your support acts like a spell,
I feel calm even when I am burning in hell.
Who keeps a count of the stabs to heart each day?
Can the end only ensure that sins are washed away?

87. Society

The World is indebted
to the same people they overlooked.
Voices of support, songs of praises
echo throughout Motherlands.
Are the emotions deep-rooted?
Or is this a phase that will pass?
The humans branded untouchable for ages,
Will anyone thank him, shake his hand?

88. Special

I look at you with many wonders,
as how different you seem to be.
Two lives hovering over the Earth,
of different traits but in unity.
I wish to hold your hand like this till I exist.
I wish to be good to a lot of souls and you top the list.

89. Star

So far away yet your warmth
touches the heart of mine.
Your presence guides me
prayers help me shine.
Every day I'm elated when I find you
thinking about, looking over me.
One day I'll reach you
disintegrate & merge to be One.

90. Stop

Stay back! Take not a step further
Or your mind will explode
with the constant ill thoughts about the existence
each second you erode
and as the proud mountains
you'll one day seize to exist
Be humble and kind instead of to people as in return
they will cherish your presence and in absence, you will be
missed.

91. Stranded

Loss of words, unnerving pain,
sudden chills, diluted strength.
Shadows & reflections of a ghost,
gloom, sorrow, despair at length.
With a need for support, a faint desire to fight,
waiting for days but not a soul in sight.

92. Sublime

The white witch, Artist's muse,
whose command I dare not refuse,
or float through time and meet my end.
You deciphered the World for me,
Only with you, I wish to be,
My dear, for me thou art God sent.

93. Sun

Blazing with all its might,
the beacon of hope, and energy.
The force behind the existence of numerous living beings,
including all of humanity.
The constant motivator and guide
through life's innings.
It teaches us that the good or the worst will set one day,
and give rise to new beginnings.

94. Surprises

• 94 •

The world is full of surprises
Some good for self, some for some other.
But it never defines you or forecasts.
It just exists for fun.
It appears as a test meant to strengthen,
unlike fear which keeps you on the run.

95. Time

I am unable to recollect the exact incidents
which occurred long back on this day
I wish to visualize our first interaction in detail,
as my soul withers away.
But I kind of have the notion
It must be something wonderful
A thought that would cheer you across time
And the love would touch your soul as it did mine.

96. Time Machine

If only I had a time machine,
I would've held on to you the first time.
When you asked me to go away,
I moved away, fell in love but for my assumptions I fled.
No amount of repentance helped,
You saved me from myself again one day
Again, one day I made a new sin
while trying to repent for my mistakes.
I left my savior alone,
I was lost & in eternal pain all over again.

97. Together

Together is a dream,
Dream to live, touch the skies.
Together is a smile
Pasted on my lips as time flies.
Together is an art
Priceless, mine n never to be sold.
Together is us
In a fight, cuddling & growing old.

98. Tough

Yesterday I dived into the Hell,
and resurfaced in heaven now.
The night spent sleepless
seems to be of worth somehow.
I wish I could explain the bliss after the pain.
I don't mind the toil, just want to feel safe again.

99. Tug of War

How deep is your pain?
How big is your heart?
Does your inner self calm you down?
Or something inside tries to tear you apart?
Focus on self to face the World,
Through faith, one can challenge the herald!

100. Turbulence

Strange rituals of the mind,
sometimes to self it is unkind.
Poking at truths well versed,
knowing you can't reverse the moment you were cursed.
It is up to you to make amends,
Honest starts always meet righteous ends.

101. Unknown

I see you idling,

making sense of thoughts, sight, and sound

hiding from the world, waiting to be found.

Why don't we choose another game to play?

take some time out, and together spend the day.

Take a break for the Earth will go on.

The weight of the world need not be yours alone.

102. Virtue

In haste, one loses control.
Rightfully, patience is a virtue.
Negative clouds cluttered minds,
the situation makes false seem true.
Then do you stick together or
start tumbling like dominoes?
Even after seeing my worst,
thank you for not letting go!

103. War

A man is asked to quit brooding over
as relatively nothing ever lasts,
past a given time.
So, do I live in peace or fight for mine,
thinking of owning it all and becoming a true King
and after my last defeat, again start from the beginning?

104. White

You are a hard soul to find,
Even Herculean it is, to look up to you.
Need your help to lighten things up,
to relive a few bright days.
I fail to recall,
the first time you lost your essence,
the first time we parted ways.

105. Wife

I lie down and look at the sky,
and from the corner of my eye
escapes a tear.
It trickles down my cheek
due to the joy you provide in days so bleak.
Also, there exists a sense of sorrow and fear.
A thought of loss and the pain in life.
How blessed I am to have you as my wife!

106. Will

Born a pile of dust,
today there stands a mountain,
home to over a thousand beings
Once scared of getting washed away,
and forgotten in the ocean bed,
today it is the soul of many streams.
A scary humble and rough start,
has less effect on the strong-willed and pure at heart.

107. Worth

High up in the mountains,
gasping to catch a breath.
Blood from the forehead blinds the eye,
undiluted focus, hand firm on the sheath.
The last chance to prove your worth
to be the person you wished to be
The Grim reaper gives you the choice,
awaits his turn out of respect.
While you slowly March towards victory,
with every offering to Death.

108. Yearning

Chaos since morning,
but the memories started with you.
Yesterday's lists were done & checked,
still, I stay sleep-deprived, dream-wrecked.
To make you stay, I am yearning,
at least will end my thoughts with you.